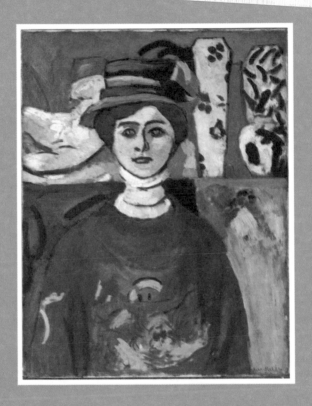

Paris Portraits

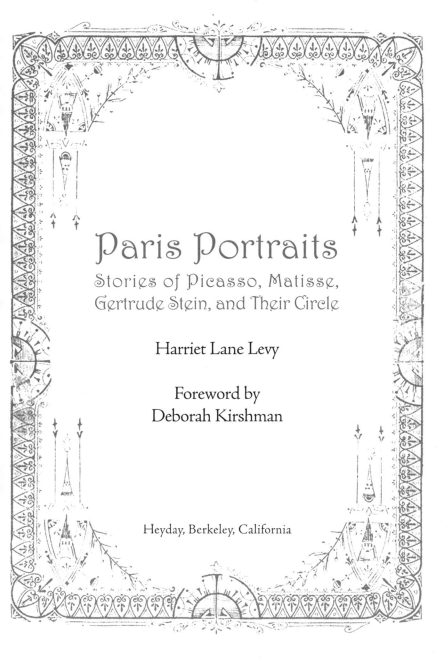

Paris Portraits
Stories of Picasso, Matisse, Gertrude Stein, and Their Circle

Harriet Lane Levy

Foreword by
Deborah Kirshman

Heyday, Berkeley, California

With gratitude to Michael McCone for his generous support of this book

This manuscript (BANC MSS C-H 11, Harriet Lane Levy recollections) is reproduced by permission from The Bancroft Library, University of California, Berkeley.

Foreword © 2011 Deborah Kirshman

Endpapers:
Henri Matisse, *La fille aux yeux verts* (The Girl with Green Eyes), 1908. Oil on canvas, 26 inches x 20 inches (66.04 cm x 50.8 cm), San Francisco Museum of Modern Art, Bequest of Harriet Lane Levy. © 2010 Succession H. Matisse/Artists Rights Society (ARS), New York.

Henri Matisse, French, 1869–1954, *Blue Nude: Memory of Biskra*, 1907. Oil on canvas, 36.25 x 55.25 inches (92.1 x 140.4 cm), The Baltimore Museum of Art: The Cone Collection, formed by Dr. Claribel Cone and Miss Etta Cone of Baltimore, Maryland, BMA 1950.228. Photography by Mitro Hood. © 2010 Succession H. Matisse/Artists Rights Society (ARS), New York.

Library of Congress Cataloging-in-Publication Data

Levy, Harriet Lane.
  Paris portraits : stories of Picasso, Matisse, Gertrude Stein, and their circle / Harriet Lane Levy ; foreword by Deborah Kirshman.
     p. cm.
  ISBN 978-1-59714-157-4 (hardcover : alk. paper)
  1. Levy, Harriet Lane. 2. Levy, Harriet Lane--Friends and associates. 3. Stein, Gertrude, 1874-1946. 4. Picasso, Pablo, 1881-1973. 5. Matisse, Henri, 1869-1954. 6. Women authors, American--France--Paris--Biography. 7. Artists--France--Paris--Biography. 8. Intellectuals--France--Paris--Biography. 9. Paris (France)--Biography. 10. Paris (France)--Intellectual life--20th century. I. Title.
  DC705.L48A3 2011
  700.92'244361--dc22

                              2010052689

Book Design: Lorraine Rath
Printing and Binding: Thomson-Shore, Dexter, MI

Orders, inquiries, and correspondence should be addressed to:
          Heyday
          P.O. Box 9145, Berkeley, CA 94709
          (510) 549-3564, Fax (510) 549-1889
          www.heydaybooks.com

10 9 8 7 6 5 4 3 2 1

Contents

Foreword: "I Lived between the Passions of the Steins"

Deborah Kirshman

When she died in 1950, Harriet Lane Levy left the San Francisco Museum of Art a trove of art.* The chef-d'oeuvre of her gift is one of Matisse's most ravishing early paintings, *La Fille aux Yeux Verts* (The Girl with Green Eyes, 1908). Rendered with vibrant, joyous color, the young woman confronts the viewer with self-assurance. Although the painting is not a portrait of Levy, it serves as a window into understanding this fiercely independent woman—a talented writer and a lover of the arts—whose long life spanned the Gilded Age and much of the modern era.

Until now, *Paris Portraits: Stories of Picasso, Matisse, Gertrude Stein, and Their Circle* has never been published in its entirety. It has long been a resource for art historians and Gertrude Stein scholars, but these remembrances—

---

* The San Francisco Museum of Art added "modern" to its name in 1975, becoming the San Francisco Museum of Modern Art.

refreshing, illuminating, and poignant—of a San Franciscan's time among the most celebrated avant-garde artists and writers of the early twentieth century have for the most part rested, unnoticed by the world at large, in the collections of UC Berkeley's Bancroft Library for decades. Their publication now will provide readers not only with an authentic portrait of the pathbreakers of modernism, but of a woman of great intelligence, insight, and wit.

One of three daughters, Harriet was born in 1867 to an upper-middle-class Jewish couple in San Francisco, Benish and Yetta Levy. Her early life was marked by tradition—young Jewish women were cloistered in their homes until they married, and finding an appropriate husband was the utmost goal and indeed the only acceptable option. Harriet defied convention, however, and in the face of prejudices against educated women, she became the first in her family to gain a college education. At age sixteen she left 920 O'Farrell Street each day to ferry across the bay to attend the University of California. Upon graduation in 1886, she followed her dreams and became a journalist when few women were in the profession. She worked for the weekly San Francisco publication *The Wave*—whose illustrious writers included Jack London and Frank Norris—and later she was hired as the drama critic

for the *Call*, considered the best San Franciscan newspaper at that time.*

About twenty years later, Harriet set off for France, a trip inspired by two women she knew from her early days on O'Farrell Street: her next-door neighbor, Alice Babette Toklas, and Sarah Samuels. She recounts in *Paris Portraits* that it all began with a fortune-teller, who foretold Sarah's marriage to Michael Stein, director of the Omnibus Railroad and Cable Company. Soon after the fulfillment of this prediction, Sarah and Michael were living part-time in Paris with Michael's siblings Leo and Gertrude Stein. During a trip home to survey their property after the 1906 earthquake, Sarah invited Alice and Harriet to visit them in Paris, and at age forty, Harriet chose Parisian adventure over Victorian spinsterhood. She would have to lend Alice one thousand dollars for the trip, but Alice was persuasive: "At worst it would be more diverting to sit behind a window in Paris and see life go by than to observe it from an apartment in San Francisco."

Harriet and Alice arrived in Paris in 1907, the year Picasso painted his revolutionary *Les Demoiselles d'Avignon* and Matisse his sensational *Blue Nude: Memory of Biskra*. The two women shared an apartment and were

---

* Levy's early life is chronicled in her charming memoir *920 O'Farrell Street: A Jewish Girlhood in Old San Francisco* (Doubleday, 1947; Heyday Books, 1997).

introduced to Gertrude Stein and her vibrant circle of avant-garde artists, writers, musicians, collectors, and dealers. In *Paris Portraits* Harriet presents a priceless array of anecdotes to describe her firsthand encounters with these colorful personalities. On one occasion, for example, she finds herself at a supper in Montmartre honoring Henri Rousseau, with the Steins, Picasso, Fernande Olivier (Picasso's mistress), Georges Braque, Marie Laurencin, Guillaume Apollinaire, and the poet André Salmon. Upon realizing there isn't enough food, the men scramble to pull together a meal; then, with Braque playing accordion and Leo Stein accompanying him on the violin, an exuberant celebration begins. When Picasso asks Harriet to sing a song from America, she responds with a rousing rendition of the Cal Oski Yell.

Most illuminating is that four Jewish women from the San Francisco Bay Area—Gertrude Stein, Sarah Stein, Alice B. Toklas, and Harriet Levy—played a significant role in the Parisian avant-garde as artists, collectors, supporters, and hostesses of salons. During the Steins' weekly salons, which were key to advancing artists' careers, Gertrude expounded on the genius of Picasso while Sarah argued for the preeminence of Matisse. Harriet describes the overpowering personalities of the two Stein women and their effect on her: "I lived

between the passions of the Steins…I felt that the two factions had identified their authority with the identity of the two painters…I was afraid of [Gertrude's] contempt, but I was more afraid of Sarah's anger…That is why I have only Matisses."

Harriet learned, not without effort, to appreciate modern art and grew to love Matisse's paintings. She wrote about the intense emotions they evoked: "I understood what he was giving, the decree of a love that he was trying to communicate. It gave me a key to all his paintings… [it was] the kindling in me of an intensity that I had never seen in nature." Through the Steins' close relationship with Matisse, Harriet gained the privilege of first selection. She purchased *La Fille aux Yeux Verts* when it was still wet and unsigned—outmaneuvering the Russian art collector "Stronkine" (probably Sergei Shchukin), who wanted to purchase the same painting.

Characterizing Gertrude Stein as impatient with those who didn't appreciate her writings, Harriet admitted that she couldn't understand them at first and distrusted people who took pleasure in them. "I believed that because they accepted her authority they were overjoyed when they understood a line, and loudly published their satisfaction and exaggerated their own appreciation." Eventually, though, she became a devotee, describing Gertrude's writing as "vivisectional"—"as if

emotions were revealing themselves in their original state of being."

Harriet's and Alice's lives changed dramatically after they joined the Steins in Fiesole in the summer of 1908, and *Paris Portraits* vividly exposes aspects of Gertrude Stein's personality and personal life at this time. Alice fell hopelessly in love with Gertrude, weeping uncontrollably and using thirty handkerchiefs a day. Meanwhile, Sarah Stein, who had turned to the Christian Science faith, began counseling Harriet. When Harriet told Gertrude that the new faith helped her walk better after eight years of distress, Gertrude was "bothered by the fact that there had been no change in me, no transformation in my character, just the miraculous fact of my being able to walk." Harriet felt the weight of Gertrude's "ponderous judgments," but she also valued the growth in her appreciation of art under Gertrude's guidance. When she visited a gallery in Florence with Gertrude, the art would "release a beauty invisible to me when I went alone."

As Gertrude and Alice grew closer, Harriet began to feel more isolated, squeezed out of her friendship with Alice. Gertrude's dislike of Harriet and desire for her to leave came out in a mean-spirited word portrait, "Harriet," in which she mocks Harriet's indecision about returning home: "She said she did not have any plans for the summer. No one was interested in this thing in

whether she had any plans for the summer. That is not the complete history of this thing…She had not made plans for the summer and she had not made plans for the following winter."*

Harriet returned to San Francisco without Alice in 1910. During a subsequent visit to Paris, Harriet was anxious to show Gertrude her writings, but Gertrude preempted her: "I am great," Gertrude said. When Harriet retorted, "But you were great fifteen years ago," Gertrude replied, "No, that was only to the English-speaking people. Now France knows and honors me." Harriet recounts this illustration of Gertrude's inflated ego with sardonic wit and with a sense of her own value. She understood her place in the Steins' pantheon, or perhaps lack of place. Having returned to San Francisco at forty-seven, she lived there for the rest of her life. Despite relationships with several suitors she never married, preferring a single life enriched by family, travel abroad, and myriad intellectual interests. Her legacy endures through her luminous writing, the exquisite art she acquired, and this unique treasure, *Paris Portraits*.

Deborah Kirshman is the former Fine Arts Editor and Assistant Director of the University of California Press.

---

* Gertrude Stein, *Portraits and Prayers* (Random House, 1934), 105–107.

I Join the Steins in Paris

It started with a fortune-teller in San Francisco.

One day my friend Sarah Samuels told me that the night before, at a fair in the Woman's City Club, a fortune-teller had told her that she was about to meet a man from Baltimore who would become important in her life. He moved among wheels, and wheels, and wheels. A month later Sarah told me that she had met a man who was interested in the United Railroads in San Francisco.

"Where'd he come from?" I asked.

"From Baltimore," Sarah said.

Sarah Samuels was a girlhood friend.

Michael Stein, his brothers, and sisters held stock in the Market Street Railroad. Michael's father had bequeathed his

share of his stock in the railroad to his children, which was the Ellis Street Branch. Because of the volume of his interest, Michael had been named Vice-President. There were many strikes in the railroad at this time. Under stones thrown by the strikers, Michael personally took out the first car from the barn. He hated all business. He wanted to get out of it. He would get out of it. He attended to the affairs of his brother Leo and his sister Gertrude, who were living in Paris. He would like to live in Paris. He married Sarah Samuels.

Furthering his plan to escape from business, he built a block of homes in the new Western residential section on Lyon Street in San Francisco. They were built under the design of Arthur Mathews, a local architect of ability and originality. They were duplex houses, shingled, novel in San Francisco. They commanded a good rental.

His money converted into stable rental property, Michael prepared to embark upon his own mode of living. He would escape, for the remainder of his days, from dependence upon salary and enjoy freedom in a foreign city, living according to his own pleasure. The block of houses was rented and the Steins left San Francisco for Paris.

When Alice Toklas, who was my next-door neighbor on O'Farrell Street, came to me and suggested our going to Europe together, I gave a distress in my shoulder of long standing as a reason for my not leaving home. Alice argued

Alice B. Toklas photographed by Arnold Genthe, 1906. Courtesy of The Bancroft Library, University of California, BANC PIC 1964.049f—AX.

that at worst it would be more diverting to sit behind a window in Paris and see life go by than to observe it from an apartment in San Francisco.

Alice too had her arguments for not going. She had been living beyond her means, supporting new social relationships with people of wealth. Not only did she not have money, she was in debt. She still owed money for the purchase of a set of silver fox which she felt it imperative to possess for some social occasion. She couldn't leave home with that debt hanging over her. If she could borrow money…?

At that stage I remembered that I had a thousand dollars saved in the Wells Fargo Bank. I would loan it to her. I asked my nephew, a lawyer, how that could be arranged. He dictated a form of a note which I gave to Alice. The distress in my shoulder continued to trouble me, but we went to Paris.

We chose Paris for our destination because the Steins were already established there in a world unknown to them before. They had settled among a group of young artists trying out their new ideas.

Sarah was my friend, and I had known Gertrude and Leo in Florence. I never asked if I would be welcome; I never questioned the right to intimacy but came to rue Madame as if I were an expected guest. We wrote of our planned visit, and we were there.

From left: Leo Stein, Allan Stein, Gertrude Stein, Therese Ehrman, Sarah Stein, Michael Stein, 1904. Courtesy of The Bancroft Library, University of California, BANC PIC 1992.078.5:7a.

Everybody seemed happy to welcome us and help us get placed. We stepped right into the heart of the Latin Quarter. We walked into a hotel on the Boulevard Saint-Michel and in a day we felt ourselves to be a part of the life of the Quarter.

We looked to the Steins for information, guidance of every kind. What Mike and Sarah did not have to give us in the way of guidance, Leo and Gertrude gave. We never questioned our right to demand it. They were there to give; we to receive.

If we were not relatives, we were friends. We took

for granted that they would introduce us to their circle of friends. We didn't question our adequacy to occupy a position, a place, among them.

* * *

The first night when we dined with them, Leo turned to me and asked, "Are you a monist?"

I had no idea what a monist was. Nor did I feel called upon to defend my ignorance. I said, "No, I am not a monist."

Alice said nothing, she looked into space. And I looked into space.

Even now I don't know if I was being teased.

I thought a monist must be something people knew about in Paris, in this new world into which I had come. You had the right to be one or not to be one. No detriment to your standing attached itself to you in either case.

So I said (only), "No, I am not a monist," and waited for the next question.

I was not embarrassed because I did not know.

All I knew was that here was one of the questions that they put to you and that someday I would know what it was that I was not.

I just remained silent, and Alice remained silent.

I thought that the question was of the same order as that put to me by Zangwill when I had visited him in

England some years ago. He had asked me if I was a Zionist. I didn't know then what a Zionist was, as I did not know now what a monist was.

I remember that my lack of knowledge was not attended by any embarrassment to me.

These people just asked questions and did not seem to place importance upon your answer.

Were you something
     or
were you *not* something.
They asked
And you said
Yes
     or
No
And that was the end of it.
It was very simple.
I know that I was not a monist and I said so.
It was a world to be at ease in.

No consequence hung upon what you told, upon what you said.

Now I said I was no monist and waited for more conversation.

We went back to the large room and looked at the paintings of Matisse and Picasso on the walls.

Leo waited to hear what we would have to say or ask. We had never heard of either artist.

I had nothing to say.

I just looked.

I was comfortable and did not feel that anything was expected of me.

I felt that in time I would get to know what it was all about.

If I was threatened by embarrassment from these surroundings into which I did not fit because of ignorance, the danger was removed almost from the beginning.

The next night when we went to dinner at the Mike Steins, one of the guests asked me where I came from. I said San Francisco. All faces turned to me with curiosity and interest.

"Were you there during…during the earthquake?"

When I said yes, questions awoke in all the eyes.

"You were in San Francisco at the time of the earthquake?"

"Yes," we said, "we were there."

In a moment we had become guests of importance. Everybody listened to us. We had something to say that interested them. Our knowledge of the recent earthquake was an accomplishment. We knew something that everybody wanted to know about.

Suddenly we were at home.

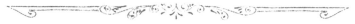

At once we became "Friends of the Steins who had been through the earthquake in San Francisco."

Any sense of inadequacy, of being in an intellectual world beyond our background, left us.

We had become at home in Paris, as we had been in California.

We found ready tongues. We ventured into a foreign language and accepted our admission into the intellectual world of Europe as our right. I saw immediately that having been in San Francisco during the earthquake was a distinction, almost an accomplishment. Now we were asked question after question.

Had we been in our house when the earthquake came?

I regretted that we had not.

However:

Our house was burned, and in the hotel in which I happened to be that night, celebrated singers of the Metropolitan Opera had been guests. I told stories of them. The celebrated singers were gathered around me on the sidewalk. Mühlmann the baritone asked me, his voice strained with fear and amazement, "Gott in Himmel, was ist denn?" and looked up at the sky as a plausible place from which such a catastrophe might be expected at any time.

At that moment the Japanese king's coat which Mühlmann was wearing impressed me as singularly right, as

a fitting costume for the reception of an early-morning earthquake in San Francisco.

Now Leo and Gertrude looked upon us with approval. We had established ourselves as objects of interest worthy to be presented at their table.

We lived on it for weeks.

However, a day came when I said to Alice, "I fear that we shall have to add something to our earthquake experience if we hope to maintain our position."

"We may even have to be burned with the house," Alice suggested.

However, we were not driven to this extremity.

Another act of God, and our prestige had ended.

The earthquake of Messina shocked the world.

San Francisco, its earthquake and its fire, were old stuff.

Visitors from Montmartre

very Thursday they came to my apartment and perched on my couch (like) three little birds. They all had the same sort of face, tight, lean, the same small nose, sharp little brilliant eyes, and red lips. I wondered what brought them to our apartment. Neither my friend Alice nor I spoke French fluently enough to make real conversation, yet they seemed happy to be with us, listening to us with the quiet attention that all our French acquaintances brought to our strained effort to make ourselves understood. They spoke of what they were doing, of what their husbands were doing, of their plans of travel for the summer, of Picasso, and Fernande, and how foolish it was of Fernande to sulk and sulk. After all, Picasso was

doing the best he could. Fernande was always like that. Always complaining. Always dissatisfied.

All we had to talk about was the friends we had in common. And the Independents Salon, where the husbands were exhibiting. Gilberte was not feeling well. She spoke of the trouble in her throat. It hurt her to swallow. Gilberte was having trouble with her husband. She was tired of trying to please him. Someday she would put an end to it. Gilberte and Clothilde looked about questioningly. I did not know what they were seeking. They looked about my apartment and sat entrenching themselves amongst the cushions. I never knew why they came, tho I liked their being there. They were Montmartre at its ease, and I had just come from San Francisco.

It was a time when rouge signified "fancy lady" to San Francisco, my city, and the frankness of their carmined cheeks, the ease of their relation to their lovers had French flavor for me. Before they left, acting as if on a simultaneous impulse, they would go to the mirror for the last line of red upon their lips. "You do not use rouge, Mlle?" they asked. "You should. It makes you feel cheerful."

Some days Gilberte came alone. She was on her way to the hospital. She was paying her daily visit to the hospital, to Charcot's clinic. She confessed her fear of cancer. She was alone. She was starving. She couldn't swallow. She had left her husband. God, how he bored her!

Every day the same conversation. After all, there is a limit. She believed that she was dying. I tried to cheer her. She grew worse and worse. I concluded that she was dying. I worried about her.

A week later she came into my house, her face glowing. Her cheeks were blown out, her eyes shining, the straight red line of confidence upon her lips. She could eat everything. A completely happy Gilberte. Again she had become a little bird perched on the bough, chirping with Montmartre gossip.

"How wonderful you look!" I cried.

She shrugged her shoulder. "You think so?"

"What has happened to Gilberte?" I asked of Clothilde when next I saw her.

"You haven't heard? She has a new ami."

"But the cancer?"

Clothilde smiled.

"Gone," she said.

The Two Camps

Every morning Alice and I went to Fernande's for a
French lesson.

Fernande was the mistress of Picasso.

They were hard-pressed for money and Gertrude
thought that anything we might pay would help them
meet their bills.

Fernande was not in the least interested in the two
American girls. She was a handsome voluptuous-looking
young woman, interested in her own life and the doings of
her friends.

It was hard for us to make conversation, for we had no
common subjects of interest. We talked of our friends the
Steins, and of the poodles in the park. How we happened

Picasso and Fernande at Montmartre, 1906. Musée Picasso Paris. Photo Credit: Réunion des Musées Nationaux/Art Resource, NY

to light on the poodles I do not know, but they were the daily subject of our conversation.

If Alice saw a poodle in the park that morning it seemed to be all that she needed to start a conversation. Fernande talked of French poodles, Alice of some poodles she had seen in San Francisco.

I remained silent. I hated poodles.

Fernande was bored. She shook her earrings and gaped.

For some reason the conversation seemed sufficiently stimulating to Alice. She talked fast. The greater her ignorance of a language, the faster she talked.

When we returned home Gertrude invariably asked, "Did Fernande wear her earrings?"

The answer determined to Gertrude the state of the Picasso finances. As long as Fernande possessed her earrings she was not in need. The absence or her earrings notified the Steins that they were at the Mont de Piété in hock.

The Steins bought pictures.

Leo was one of the earliest Americans living in Paris who understood and appreciated the new painting.

Outsiders questioned the motives of the Steins. Strangers thought they were shrewd speculators to whom the acquisition of French paintings was a good investment.

This was true only in a sense.

The Steins bought paintings for an investment, but also because they liked them.

Sarah and Michael Stein studio, 56 rue Madame, c. 1911. Courtesy of The Bancroft Library, University of California, Elise Stern Haas family photographs, BANC PIC 1992.078.6:46a.

Leo discovered Matisse. Later his feelings for Matisse paled before his growing appreciation of Picasso. Picasso's drawings interested Leo. He felt great promise in them.

With Gertrude there was no question of choice. She loved Picasso. His spirit was akin to her own, and engaged her affection even up to her death.

What that great attraction was I did not rightly know. My command of French was too limited to appreciate what it was that took Gertrude's fancy. He delighted her. The pleasure he gave her went beyond his work, it lay in

his personality. My limited understanding of French was a handicap and I was very slow in improving it.

Leo and Gertrude turned wholeheartedly to Picasso, while Sarah continued to be exclusively a Matisse enthusiast.

They became two camps in the art world of Paris.

Sarah had room for only one great enthusiasm at a time and this one lasted for all time. She could not divide her enthusiasms. Having accepted Matisse, he became for her and remained for her, the one great artist. She never divided her allegiance.

Mike had confidence in Sarah's judgment and thought that it was something to be relied upon for an investment, that if she thought the paintings were good they probably were good. I don't think he thought further than that.

When Sarah visited the galleries with Leo she brought a complete enthusiasm which never left her. A single-ness of interest that was the main characteristic of her makeup.

The crowds who came to her home on Saturday night to view the paintings were received and entertained by a woman beautifully gowned in original costumes, antique jewelry. A hostess who sat upon a couch and did not leave it, who explained the paintings on the walls, the greatness of Matisse, his unique position in the world of art. She illustrated her confidence in the expansive canvases of Matisse which covered her walls by her purchase of them.

She seemed to receive joy from the paintings. Over the years Matisse came to her for encouragement, and assurance.

Did she understand Matisse?

"Gott weiss!" I did not know.

Gertrude, who was so clear-headed, what did she think?

Even though Sarah sacrificed her life for a thing you didn't know…

I don't know that I knew a thing about her real feelings.

I do know that if I had not been enslaved by my fidelity to something which I could not understand, I would have bought the whole bunch of her Picassos, which gave me genuine pleasure.

Sarah should have been analyzed.

After a lifetime of intimacy I felt that I did not know her.

I think that she had emotional reactions of great insight. But never a recognition of her own weaknesses. She had an incapacity to accept criticism and wasted her energy in self-defense, until the critic, weary of the futility of his job, gave up opposition and pretended to agree with her. I did that again and again until the time came when, to save time, I agreed with her immediately. Knowing that she must always, always, always be right.

I liked her very much, but was never happy with her. Because I was never honest or given the opportunity to be honest.

Some day on her road up a spiritual flight she will

pause to defend herself against a questioning of her perfection.

There is something pathetic about the richness and futility of an endowment like hers.

Endowment

Futility

Keenest observation

Sharp discrimination,

And an unbreakable wall that kept her vanity intact.

I never think of her with pleasure, or satisfaction, or confidence.

Collectors from America like Mrs. Sears said that when they were with Mrs. Stein they were hypnotized and ready to buy Matisse pictures. When they left her, demesmerized, they did not understand them or have confidence in them. They spoke of this to Mrs. Stein, who smiled as one who could sympathize with their ignorance, but as one who understood things beyond their appreciation.

Of the greatness of Matisse she had complete conviction and left everyone bewildered when she deserted art and took up the life of a Christian Science practitioner.

Nobody will ever have an explanation of that.

After a year's intensive work at the atelier of Matisse, where she painted from eight in the morning to six at night, she went to southern France to work alone.

She brought back with her every canvas that she had

painted. Matisse was delighted. He gave her work great praise.

We all believed that she was embarked upon the career of a painter and would be a good one.

To our astonishment, an interest in Christian Science, slumbering within her during the period of her intensive painting, suddenly appeared, as if it had been flowering in a secret place over the months.

Out of the nowhere she declared she would not become a painter. To be a first-class painter, as she felt she might, like ———, would take at least ten years, she said.* At that moment she felt her worth as a Christian Science practitioner was something certain and would bear immediate fruit.

In face of all the praise for her painting from Matisse, whom she had accepted and extravagantly advertised, she gave up painting and declared that she would give her life to the practice of Christian Science.

Mike consented to the change.

She rose to positions of greater and greater activity in the church. For fifteen years she practiced Christian Science. (For fifteen years she was a Christian Science practitioner.)

I lived between the passions of the Steins. Or thought I

---

* Note included in the original manuscript: "Harriet could not remember the name of the artist Sarah felt she could not be like."

did. I felt that the two factions had identified their author-ity with the identity of the two painters. This was more characteristic of Sarah than of Gertrude. Sarah's identifi-cation was more intense than Gertrude's.

Their own status was affected by the status they cre-ated for these two artists by publicizing so enthusiastically their opinions.

Sarah's defense of Matisse as he grew in prestige was not only a defense of Matisse but a defense of the ram-parts of her own judgment and authority.

I was impaled between two forces.

I was eager to own a Picasso.

I didn't dare show Sarah my interest. It would have been received as heresy to the authority of the Mike Steins, who had declared themselves for Matisse.

Nor did I tell Gertrude how much I wanted the Picassos.

I did not confess to Gertrude that I was afraid of Sarah.

Gertrude would have scorned such timidity. I was afraid of her contempt, but I was more afraid of Sarah's anger. There came a time when, had I not been afraid of Sarah, I would have bought a Picasso on her walls for fifty dollars. To this day I cannot endure my self-reproach because I did not.

The Steins were authority incarnate to me!

I spent my time avoiding the questioning of the finality of this authority. To question Sarah's supreme rightness was

to open argument upon argument that would last for days, until coercion brought with it acquiescence in the infallibility of Sarah. Rarely would one day alone achieve this result.

To question the importance of Gertrude was to evoke a blast that was annihilating.

Between these two explosions of force I picked my way.

The first exhibition came almost upon our arrival in Paris and established for us the insecurity of our tenure. Gertrude asked Alice to call on her one afternoon.

She named the hour.

Four o'clock.

We were visiting a gallery and Alice was late in keeping her appointment. When she entered Gertrude's apartment she met an outraged lioness. Gertrude, her corduroy gown flying from her, stamped up and down the room.

How had Alice dared!

To break an appointment with her.

With a woman of her importance!

Alice's apology was swept away.

It was unpardonable.

That was our introduction to the power and violence of Stein authority disregarded…

That is why I did not buy the Picassos.

Another time I was spending the summer on the Mediterranean at Trayas. The Mike Steins, Alice, and I. Sarah was to celebrate her birthday.

Harriet Levy, Sarah Stein, and Sylvia Salinger in Paris, winter 1912-13. Courtesy of The Bancroft Library, University of California, BANC PIC 1992.078.5:36.

We all went down to Cannes and bought gifts.

Early in the morning, while Sarah was still in bed, we knocked at her door to present her with our birthday gifts.

"Happy birthday," we sang in unison and entered the room together.

Sarah sat up in bed, rigid.

"This is not my birthday!"

She looked at each one of us accusingly and then at her husband.

"You didn't know that today was not my birthday? You didn't even know that about your wife? You didn't know the date of her birthday?"

Mike grinned sheepishly.

"I always thought it was today." The tissue-covered gift in his hand shook. "Never mind, never mind," he said, "we will celebrate it tomorrow."

"We will not," said Sarah. "And let the proprietor know? And let everybody in the hotel know that an American man doesn't know even the date of his wife's birthday!"

We stole out of the room one by one.

Convicted!

That was why I didn't buy the Picassos.

That is why I have only Matisses.

I was to leave Trayas before the Steins.

My regret in leaving was that I was curtailing my instruction in Christian Science by Sarah.

The night before I left I was anticipating my return to America and the pleasures that were in store for me.

"The first thing I'll do," I said, "when I have stepped off the gangplank will be to go to the theatre and see a play of George Cohan."

I glowed at the prospect.

I glanced up to see Sarah looking outraged.

"George Cohan!" she cried. "And here I have spent the whole summer establishing a spiritual consciousness for you. Wasted!"

She got up and left the room.

She hardly spoke to me from that time until I left Trayas.

Far from a spiritual consciousness was the rage that possessed me. I could not get rid of it for days in Paris.

That was a violent experience.

Sitting in the Luxembourg Gardens in Paris, trying to free myself of my desire to kill Sarah, I fought a daily battle.

Memories of this are no doubt at the basis of why I haven't the Picassos today. The lovely Picassos that used to hang on the Mike Steins' wall.

I knew no relaxation in Paris because of my relationship and the complexity of that relationship with the Steins. I would say of my whole relation to the Steins that, in spite of my affection for them, I hated them because I never had the courage to tell them to go to hell, as I so often wanted to do. I hated myself for not being able to tell them to go to hell.

The Visit of Barnes

Visitors felt the lash of Sarah's scorn. They feared to acknowledge that they could not understand. They were afraid not to consent, some of their opinions might turn out to be important. They would have liked to include themselves as one of the early messengers of a new gospel. They wished that the canvases did not offend them so painfully. They tried to like them, but for all their effort, they could not escape the suspicion that they were being hypnotized by the Steins. Once out in the open, free from the barrage of Mrs. Stein's personal charm and the fluency of her arguments, they feared a return to their freedom.

They were afraid of the brilliant canvases—of their unorthodoxy. They couldn't bear the violence of them.

They were afraid to buy them, they were afraid not to buy them. Afraid that they would turn out to be the important paintings the Steins said they were.

After all, who were these Steins? American speculators, no doubt, who were buying them in the ateliers of poor artists, who were collecting them at low prices, talking them up and later would sell them to American collectors and make a fortune.

One night a tall man came into the room and examined the walls. He stood before a large canvas, examined it for a moment, then walked across the room to Mr. Stein.

"My name is Barnes," he said. "That picture." He motioned to a large canvas over the couch, to a painting of a young nude.

"I'll take that one."

Mr. Stein followed the direction of his arm—the Picasso?

"I'll give you $5000 for it."

"We are not dealers." Mr. Stein said in the low voice habitual to him.

"Not dealers?"

"No, we are collectors."

"You don't sell? Anything?"

"No."

"What are you doing with all these paintings?"

"We enjoy them."

The visitor drew a card from his pocket. "In case you change your mind, this is my address. My name is Barnes."

Mr. Stein regarded the card with curiosity.

"I'll remember," he said and grinned.

Mr. Barnes left.

"He offered me $5000 for the Picasso." Mr. Stein said to his wife. Her merry eyes glinted.

"Did you tell him what we paid for it?" she asked.

"No. He was just getting around to ask me."

The Apartment of Leo and Gertrude

The restlessness did not come from the paintings on the wall. In spite of their strangeness it was not they that communicated to us our feeling of unrest as Leo and Gertrude walked up and down the room, their eyes repeatedly returning to the door.

"What's wrong?" I asked Gertrude when she stopped a moment in front of me.

"They may be coming at any moment," she said.

"Who?"

"Either Hapgood or Edstrom, or both. If they meet, anything can happen.*

---

* American journalist and author Hutchins Hapgood (1869–1944) and Swedish American sculptor Peter David Edstrom (1873–1938).

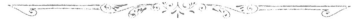

Leo caught her sentence as she passed, his eyes never leaving the door.

"Edstrom may come at any moment. Frost saw him on the train coming from Florence."

I looked from one to the other for explanation.

"Edstrom ran off with the book," Gertrude explained, her eye upon the door.

"What book?"

"The book that Hapgood was writing. The book that Edstrom was dictating to him. Edstrom had just finished it. It was ready to be published. Hutch Hapgood had been working on it for weeks. He was delighted with it. It was the story of Edstrom's life."

"Who is Edstrom?" I asked.

"The Swedish sculptor. The hope of Sweden, until his health broke," Leo said. He went to Florence to recover his health. His arm was paralyzed. He had to stop working. Hutch and Edstrom met in Florence. Hutch ate him up whole. A bad man who loved his badness, never had Edstrom had such an audience. Never a Don Juan had so perfect an audience for the recital of his conquests of the ladies of the Swedish Court. Edstrom talked. Hapgood wrote. Chapters rolled from his fountain pen, creating a volume of Boccaccio tales. Edstrom swelled into importance as he dictated. The book was practically finished. One more sitting, and it would be done. Hapgood returned

for the last sitting. He waited for Edstrom. Edstrom did not appear. He had run off from Florence with the manuscript, and had taken the last train for Paris. He left no explanation. Gertrude said that it must have come to him that the portrait which he had painted of himself was not as handsome as it seemed when he told it. Perhaps he had read the last chapter over in his hotel room and had been frightened by the picture that he had painted of himself. In print it may not have measured up as grand as when he had spoken it. At any rate he wasn't going to let it get away from him. Just spoken, he could deny that he had ever said it, deny that he had ever dictated what he said had happened. At any rate, he would escape. Under the admiration in Hapgood's eyes, being a man in high society had been an accomplishment that built up a fine stature— a stature that dwindled when he was alone.

Edstrom wrote to the Steins that he was leaving Florence and he would be in Paris. Hapgood wrote to Leo. He wrote that Edstrom had quit on the job after he, Hapgood, had given weeks to the biography that promised to be a sensation, besides being fresh and wonderfully real. Hapgood said it was sure to create a sensation, as it involved people of the highest rank of Swedish society. He was leaving Florence. He would find Edstrom and force him to return the manuscript. If Edstrom refused he would kill him. The Steins would

see him in Paris, as soon as he could pack his effects. He would shoot Edstrom on sight.

Leo declared that he must be stopped. Even if Edstrom could be induced to surrender the book, Hapgood must be prevailed upon not to publish it. Hapgood must be made to see that such a book, exposing the private lives of women known throughout Sweden, should never be published. Hapgood must not be permitted to publish the book, Leo said.

"Never," Gertrude agreed.

The door opened.

A tall, slender young blond entered the room.

It was Edstrom.

He looked from Gertrude to Leo.

"Has he been here?"

"Not yet," they said.

"I've got it with me," he said. "I won't let him have it."

"You had better leave before he gets here," Leo said. "We'll talk to him. Persuade him to give up the whole idea. Tell him it won't do at all. Tell him it should not have been written."

Edstrom laughed.

"Wouldn't do me any good," he said. "I can see that."

"I think you'd better go," Gertrude said. "Hutch may come in any minute. We will speak to him."

"You mean that I had better go now?"

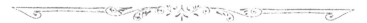

"Yes. Now, before he gets here."

Edstrom picked up his hat, waved good-bye and left.

The door closed upon him.

It opened again.

A young man entered.

It was Hapgood.

He looked around the room.

"Has he been here?"

"You cannot publish that book," Gertrude said. "Any-one but Edstrom would know that. A man doesn't betray his relations with women of such position. It isn't done."

"He loved it," Hutch said. "He couldn't tell enough. There was nothing that he wasn't ready to tell."

"I know," said Gertrude. "But you mustn't let him tell. You know better, even if he doesn't. Besides, he won't give you the story. Something is making him change his mind about telling it."

"I remember every word of it," said Hutch. "I can write it from memory. I'll find him wherever he is. If he won't give me the book I'll kill him."

Hutch rose.

Gertrude put her hand on his arm.

"Please think it over," she said. "Promise me you won't do anything until you've thought it over. You are too good to lend yourself to this sort of thing. Promise."

Hapgood rose.

"All right," he said, drawing away his arm from Gertrude's hand.

"He's a low-down dog," he muttered, and left the room. The door opened.

Edstrom was in the room.

"Was he mad?" he asked.

"He's going to find you and kill you," Leo said pleasantly.

"I hid the manuscript in the bottom of my trunk," Edstrom said.

"You had better burn it," Leo said. "It should never have been written. You must have seen that when you ran off with it. That's why you did run off. Isn't it? You saw that it never should have been written?"

Edstrom smiled slyly.

"It's mighty interesting stuff, Leo. Hutch said it is wonderful material and well written. Some day I might want to publish it myself."

He looked up and caught Leo's eye.

That was my introduction to 7 rue de Fleurus and to David Edstrom.

Gertrude Stein studio, 27 rue de Fleurus, Paris, c. 1910. Courtesy of Yale Collection of American Literature, Beinecke Rare Book and Manuscript Library.

Visit to Edstrom

Every morning I went to Edstrom's studio. He was making a portrait of me. There were many interruptions. Young art students from Sweden, to whom the name of Edstrom meant something, knocked on the door. Edstrom answered and let in the men who asked to see his work. He said coldly that he had not been producing lately, and showed them out. Then he turned to me a face distorted by anger. I felt frightened by the change in his expression. After a moment he sat down on the bench against the wall.

"It's amazing," he said.

"What's amazing?"

"The way I've changed since I've come into Christian

Science. If this had happened to me six months ago I would have smashed your portrait. Now, see how calm I am."

He returned to the portrait, distorted it by his turbulent feelings.

After a little he said, "You have an awful effect on me. Every morning I begin to work in the highest frame of mind. I read a chapter from the gospel of St. John and feel myself exalted. Then you come here and force me to tell you a story about some damn woman in Sweden or Venice. My spiritual sense is gone. Sometimes I can't get it back all morning. You have a terrible effect on a man. Every time my thoughts are high you drag them down."

He returned to my portrait, which had taken on an expression quite different from the one of yesterday.

The postman was knocking.

Edstrom rose and walked to the door.

"Are you expecting a letter?" I asked.

"Who knows? It might be a check," he said.

"Anybody owing you anything?"

"No, nobody. But you never can tell."

He returned to the portrait.

"I've been thinking about you," he said. "I bet I know all about you, what kind of a person you are."

He looked up from the portrait.

He looked as though he had just unearthed a great discovery about me.

"I bet you have the same friends that you had when you were a girl."

"I have," I said. "What's wrong about that?"

"Nothing," he said and looked triumphant. "I was just thinking that you would be just that kind of a person. My wife was like that. Her people were Jewish. The way my wife worshipped her parents was something awful to live with. I couldn't stand it. The older her relatives were, the higher was her regard for them. Sometimes when we were living in their home I couldn't stand it. I would take the best-known whore in the city to dine at the best hotel in the city just to show the family of my wife what I thought of them. The whole bunch of them."

"I don't think so much of that," I said.

"You wouldn't," he said. "You Jews are all alike."

Edstrom

Gertrude wrote portraits of Edstrom, changing them from day to day. He fascinated her. Day after day she made new portraits of him.

I couldn't read Gertrude's writings. I couldn't understand them. I distrusted those who found pleasure in them. I believed that because they accepted her authority they were overjoyed when they understood a line, and loudly published their satisfaction and exaggerated their own appreciation.

Gertrude said I couldn't understand her because I read her with prejudiced eyes, because I listened to her with prejudiced ears. She said the young could understand her because they were free.

One night I was sitting in her apartment at a table reading a volume of her portraits. I read a portrait of Edstrom.

Everlastingly she was making portraits of Edstrom.

As I read I became excited. I was experiencing a sense of life such as I had never before experienced in reading.

What I was experiencing was not photographic. It was not representation. It was vivisectional. It was as if emotions were revealing themselves in their original state of being.

Never before had I experienced such living feeling.

It was a new sense of life in the living.

I said to Gertrude, "What is this that I am experiencing that I have never experienced before? Is all your writing like this?"

She said, "Yes. Just as you are feeling it in this one paragraph, so other people are feeling it in others. I must conclude that it is everywhere, recognizable according to the individual perception of the reader."

I did not feel it again. But the impression of that vivisectional emotion was so vivid that I was never able to negate it.

Later, I again felt such an intense emotion before a few canvases of Matisse.

Again it was a sense of life in the living.

To Gertrude, Edstrom was a multiple personality.

When I went to his studio I never knew which personality would greet me.

Some days when I entered the studio I was afraid of the man who sat on the floor, his straight blonde hair hanging heavily over his forehead excluding half-closed eyes, charged, with evil. Sitting on the floor I thought of Saul on the floor of his tent. The words which came from his lips were charged with malevolence.

Another time his eyes would be clear, his hair golden, he stood tall and straight, his thought touched by some super-insight, lifting me in its flight to reaches I had never known. He was seeing a beauty that bore me to high places.

David Edstrom, 10 April 1922. Courtesy of the Library of Congress, Prints and Photographs Division, LC-DIG-npcc-22838.

He didn't recognize these changes in himself. He could rise high and fall low and never know the difference. That was the trouble with his work. He didn't know when he hadn't sustained himself and he resisted criticism.

He might have been a great sculptor if he had recognized this.

One day he showed me a small torso of a woman that I liked very much. I told him that I thought it had a lyrical beauty.

He said, "There you go. You tell me that you know nothing about art and you know more than most people."

He returned it to a cabinet and brought forth a figure with spread wings. He said it was meant to be placed in a garden, in the open. I said I didn't care for it. It wasn't creative.

"A woman always has her limitations," he said and returned it to the cabinet.

He was in love with Cora Downer. She was the Christian Science practitioner sent by the church in Boston to introduce Christian Science to Europe. A tall regal woman of aristocratic bearing. As a child she had been blind and had been taken to many oculists of authority in Europe. Back in Boston she found herself in the office of a Christian Science practitioner, her mother's last hope. The practitioner spoke, and the little girl thought, What a fool to think that she is going to do anything for me.

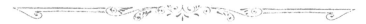

As she thought, her blindness was lifted from her and she saw. After that day she became absorbed in the study of Christian Science and gradually took up the practice of it.

In Paris she established a branch of the Christian Science church, healed the sick, and taught Christian Science.

Edstrom, his arm paralyzed by a stroke, came to her for help. In a short time he recovered the use of his arm and entered her class for instruction.

She had never met anyone like him. None of her standards were sacred to him. He told her she was ignorant. She knew nothing about art and he spoke to her from a standpoint of a superiority that ignored all her own values.

He disrupted her classes. She dismissed him from the class but agreed to see him after the class sessions.

She ended by falling in love with him.

Art represented a completely new world to her. She had no understanding of it and felt in it something superior. Her ignorance gave her a conviction of inferiority to Edstrom. Her high estimates of her own values dwindled under the contempt of this sculptor and his appraisal of her. She was overwhelmed by the authority of the art world of Paris, in which she found all her standards ignored.

Gradually she accepted Edstrom's valuation of himself, having no way of questioning (testing) its validity. She saw herself contributing to his greatness. She saw his talent as

a gift of God. She would assist in an act of creation. She saw herself kindling the creative urge in him. She would help open the door to inspiration. She would help establish an artist in the realm of his greatness.

She never thought to question the limit or strength of his endowment. She took him upon his own valuation. He presented to her an opportunity to help genius unfold. She had seen physical strength reestablish itself in his paralyzed arm. In like manner she would see the strength of the spirit appear in his sculpture.

She married him.

Postscript

During Cora Downer's marriage to Edstrom a friend of mine met the two of them at dinner in Berlin. My friend was a professor at the University of California. He told me that she seemed artificial in an intellectual environment, trying to adjust herself to a world of which she was proud, but a world into which she did not fit.

Later I heard that her health was failing. Then, that her early blindness had returned, and at the last that she had died prematurely.

The end of her tragic marriage.

Portrait: Drives in the Bois

In the afternoon when Edstrom and I would be driving in the Bois, he often chuckled at a thought.

I asked him of what he was thinking.

He said, "I was just thinking how your father saved his money so carefully so that I might drive in the Bois."

The Toad: I See the Paintings

every Saturday night I went either to Gertrude's or to Sarah's to see the crowds come to view the paintings. At Sarah's one saw Matisse almost exclusively.

The high walls of the Lutheran church which the Mike Steins had converted into an apartment were covered by very large canvases by Matisse. I had never before seen such glowing color, such living color.

People came from all over the world to see them.

This was the only place where one could see them.

They remained for a short time and returned to their own countries, bearing a message, the message of a new idea, a new vision that was opening to the world.

It was mediaeval-like, recalling to me the days of

Sarah and Michael Stein studio, 56 rue Madame, c. 1912. Courtesy of The Bancroft Library, University of California, Elise Stern Haas family photographs, BANC PIC 1992.078.6:44.

Abelard and Heloise. So had new forms of religion been spread around the world.

Little groups came from Russia, from Norway and Sweden, from Italy, from America.

They studied in the atelier of a new artist, accepted his vision, then returned with it to their own country.

I had a feeling of being present at the birth and dissemination of a new Idea.

The room was full of discussion, of serious rebellion.

People said, "A child's work. Any child could do that."

Only Gertrude roared with laughter, a laughter that shook the ceiling.

People were angry.

Angry at Leo.

At what they called his arrogance.

Going home one night from the Steins', a young American artist complained that Leo could have treated him with greater courtesy. He could have explained what this new business was, instead of making him feel himself to be an ignoramus. He almost wept in protest. His name was Leo Simonson. He had come from America, eager for fresh enlightenment.

I saw nothing to praise in all these paintings on the walls. I was aware only of violence and abuse of everything that I had ever seen painted. Nothing in me offered discrimination between one painting and another. I looked at them over and over again, waiting for the day when they would explain themselves to me. I did not want to hear explanations of their importance, of their difference from other paintings. I wanted the paintings to explain themselves. Sarah sat on the couch in the corner explaining to everybody the greatness of Matisse. People listened to her, unconvinced, but overwhelmed by her enthusiasm and authority. I did not know what I was waiting for. I knew only that I didn't want what

Leo Stein, 27 rue de Fleurus, 1905. Courtesy of The Bancroft Library, University of California, BANC PIC 1992.078.8:64.

I was hoping for to come to me in a book or through Sarah's emphatic expositions.

Nothing happened.

Then one night Sarah and I sat alone in the corner of the gallery, Sarah on the couch, I opposite her. We were reading a new volume of the verses of Tagore which we had bought that day.

On the wall above Sarah hung a painting which Bernhard Berenson, the authority on Florentine art, had called "The Toad."

It was the picture of a woman with an extravagantly large bosom, antagonizing in its voluptuousness.

Berenson had said to Mrs. Stein, "If you can ever convince me of any beauty in that toad, I'll believe in Matisse."

I shared his opinion.

I had never been able to look up directly and accept the impact of her ugliness, her vulgarity.

Tonight we were reading Tagore. We read on and on, lifted by the power of the Spirit.

I looked up at the Matisse.

Something had happened to the painting. No longer was I looking upon heavy breasts, exaggerated, vulgar. Instead I was aware of a Giving, (of a Giving Out) so generous, so universal, of something beyond any Giving I had ever experienced.

It moved me as I had never before been moved, by the extent of its grandeur, its beauty. Here was love. Love without measure.

Now I was understanding Matisse.

I understood love as he was presenting it. I understood what he was giving, the decree of a love that he was trying to communicate.

It gave me a key to all his paintings.

After that I was never satisfied that I had *seen* a painting of Matisse until I had experienced an emotion equal to his superlative intensity. Only five times after that did

Henri Matisse photographed by Edward Steichen, undated. Courtesy of Yale Collection of American Literature, Beinecke Rare Book and Manuscript Library.

I repeat the experience, but I knew it was always there to be experienced. And I was content to wait patiently until I became aware of what was before my eyes.

Later, when Matisse spoke to me of the tranquility that he was forever seeking to achieve in his painting, I understood something of what he was trying to communicate.

I understood, too, what other painters were attempting to communicate. And even when they lacked success, respected their ideal.

To me it was the enlargement of a horizon. The kindling in me of an intensity that I had never seen in nature. Sometimes it was a realization of power, of abstract power, beyond any I had ever seen expressed in natural figure or even in a tree. In fact, I saw that the artist was searching within himself for the emotion of which he was not yet fully aware.

Two American girls came to Paris. They came to study with Matisse. Matisse asked them what they had come for. They said, "for your color." He said, "If you haven't brought your own color you will never get mine."

All the people coming to those Saturday nights talked. Their talk was full of excitement, passion, anger, rebellion. They used words whose meaning I did not understand. I never understood.

For some reason I did not ask Gertrude or Leo what they meant, not wanting to betray my ignorance. There was

nobody to ask the meaning of all I heard. So I remained quiet over months.

The night when I discovered God, I asked him. And He told me, as He told me everything else. I asked Him about this strange life I was seeing. Of the world of artists who talked a language of which I understood nothing. What was it all about? I asked God what they meant by all the strange words: the "realismus," the "idealismus." What was realismus? For answer I beheld a drawing. A drawing in black and white. A segment of light so brilliant that it was beyond all light, the shadow segment beside it was unreality. (I was told of the meaning of the artist.)

Again I asked, "What about all these people who are flocking to the new visions offered in Paris? All these excited young people who ask burning questions of Leo and Sarah?"

I did not know much, but it was enough to make me ask, "What was it that makes a man willing to surrender his own convictions?"

There was one man who did not surrender his convictions. William James, upon a visit to Gertrude's, surveyed the walls of the atelier and said, "Another world of which I know nothing."

Art Collectors (Stronkine)

O nce a week Sarah, Mike, and I accompanied Stronkine to the cellars of art dealers.*

Stronkine had taken upon himself the responsi-
bility of collecting modern French paintings for his gallery
(in Moscow). The ultimate destination of his paintings
was the gallery in the city of Moscow to which he intended
to leave his collection.

Little did he think that his benevolence would be antic-
ipated, and that his collection would be confiscated by the
city of Moscow long before his death.

---

* Stronkine is probably the Russian art collector Sergei Shchukin (1854–1936),
  whose collection was appropriated by the Russian government after the revolution,
  in 1918.

He came to Paris to select paintings, restricting his selection to works of Picasso and Matisse. The Steins had convinced him that it was between these two men that the history of French art would lie. There was never a thought that there might be other painters who would share the glory of these two men.

Our visits to the owners of contemporaneous painters were restricted to dealers in the paintings of Matisse and Picasso.

In the company of the Mike Steins, Stronkine gave his consent to the future greatness of Matisse. Every year he returned to Moscow from Paris with at least one example of the art of Matisse.

The Steins practically bought up the output of Matisse, even before they were dry. To them was given the privilege of first selection. Their claim preceded even that of Stronkine. Stronkine would buy one or two canvases, which he first exhibited in Berlin.

It they were well received, and they were for the most part, he returned to Paris and bought more.

There came a day when Matisse painted a canvas during the absence of Stronkine which the Steins and other habitual purchasers did not desire. Mike told me of it as my opportunity to possess myself of a Matisse before it had been purchased by them.

Early the next morning the Steins and I hurried to

Bernheim-Jeune to see the painting. It was *The Girl with the Green Eyes*. It was still wet and unsigned. At the same time Leo found the Renoir for which he had been waiting for many months.

We were two excited purchasers that early morning.

Mr. Fenedon, the well-known member of the Bernheim-Jeune shop, painted so often by all the great painters of the day as part of their canvases, spoke to me.*

"You are a painter, Mlle?" he asked.

"No," I answered.

"But you have a desire to paint?"

"No.

"Ah, Mlle is a sculptor?"

Again I said, "No."

"Oh, but Mlle hopes to model some day?"

Again I said, "No."

He caught my arm and pressed it.

"Remain like that, Mlle."

"Remain like that."

Leo with his Renoir returned to 7 rue de Fleurus, where he stood all night regarding his treasure.

The Girl with the Green Eyes accompanied my joyous steps to Notre Dame de Champs.

---

* Fenedon is probably the French art collector, dealer, and critic Félix Fénéon (1861–1944).

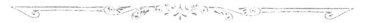

A week later the Steins brought word from Matisse. He was in a quandary. Stronkine had returned to Paris. The Matisse paintings had been a great success in Berlin. Stronkine felt justified in buying another painting. He had heard that Matisse had painted another during his absence. Where was it? It had been sold. He must have it. Matisse said it was impossible, as it had been purchased by an American woman living in Paris. He must do something about it, Stronkine insisted. Matisse told him that all he could do was to introduce him to the American woman.

It was arranged that the next Sunday morning Stronkine and the Steins and Matisse would come to my home and Stronkine would make an offer to me for my painting.

Matisse grinned when he told me about it.

He was delighted. Delighted with my surprise and reception of the prospect. The prospect of a Russian gentleman proposing to an American lady, in private life, that she sell her painting amused him greatly.

I, too, wondered how a Russian gentleman would ask an American lady to sell him one of her paintings.

Sunday morning came and with it Matisse and the two Steins to my apartment.

Then came Stronkine. He was short, white-haired, bristling. He stammered. He stood before the picture, then turned to Matisse.

"C'est…be…a…u," he stammered.

And again

"C'est excessivement beau."

Again he looked to me. "A new note. No other is like it."

He returned to the painting, then back to me. "Vous comprenez, Mlle, I have thirteen Matisses. This is a new note. This is the only one which is lacking." He paused. Again he looked at me.

I said, "M. Stronkine, I have only one Matisse. The other thirteen are lacking."

No other word was said.

I looked up to see the smiling faces of my friends.

Matisse grinned.

I said, "Je regrette."

"Je regrette," Mr. Stronkine answered.

The interview was over.

Mr. Stronkine bowed and left.

That was all.

Important Conversations
at the Steins

Picasso Squeezes the Hand of Alice

alk. Talk. And more talk.

Nothing stopped with the fact.

No matter how simple the subject, it led to further conversation.

Nothing just was.

Was it this? Or was it that? Might it not be something else?

Nothing so simple but that it was divided and subdivided.

Nothing so slight but that it warranted consideration.

It was all like that.

All talking about something. Placing something. Putting something in its proper place. Not making a mistake about it. No fact was simple. Just fact. It was something

that had to be explained, that had to be placed.

Mildred came in one morning.

"Just for a minute," she said.

Did that end it?

Not at all.

She was buying presents to send to her sister for Christmas.

She enumerated all the objects that went into the box.

I was struck particularly by the perfumed dress shields.

I had never heard of perfumed dress shields.

"Why did Mildred want to send perfumed shields to her sister?" I asked.

Perfumed shields were expensive.

She certainly did not have enough money to justify an expensive gift like that.

But Mildred was like that, they said.

She would always be.

Always extravagant.

What made her extravagant?

Or would you call it extravagant to be ample in one's generosity?

Mildred was emotional.

There were various ways of being emotional.

Did it add to Mildred or take from Mildred?

Her kind of emotion.

Was she emotional in a big way?

Picasso was emotional.

Was he emotional in the way Mildred was?

It was these differences in people that seemed to be of great importance.

They were worth a whole morning of conversation.

I couldn't see why.

But Gertrude saw why.

And so I listened attentively for greater knowledge than I had enjoyed in San Francisco. All these things that were discussed must be of great importance or Gertrude wouldn't be giving them her time. Everything that Gertrude did was important. Importance was attached to all kinds of things in Paris that were without significance in California. What made them important?

I thought about that but did not arrive at a satisfactory conclusion.

What was it that made things that happened to Steins important? Was it just because they happened to Steins? Or was it because they happened to Steins in Paris? Couldn't they have happened to other people? In that case would they still be important?

There was so much I did not know but that I hoped to learn from my friends.

For example.

One night at dinner Picasso squeezed Alice's hand under the table.

Alice reported it to Gertrude without any sense of its being of special interest. Just.

"Pablo squeezed my hand last night," Alice said.

Gertrude dropped her fork.

"Ah," said Gertrude, and she looked hard at Alice.

And she looked at me.

"Pablo squeezed my hand under the table last night," Alice repeated, and it became portentous.

Gertrude was silent. Pondering.

She looked up at Alice. "And what else?" she asked.

"Nothing," said Alice. "He just squeezed my hand."

Gertrude pondered some more.

Then she turned to me. "That could mean many things," she said. "He squeezed Alice's hand. It might have been a mere transient casual act. In that case it would have no significance. It would not be followed by any eventuality. He might have just squeezed her hand. Might even have forgotten that he had squeezed her hand after he had squeezed her hand. On the other hand," she said, and her voice became heavy with import, "if in squeezing her hand he had experienced an emotion that entered into his imagination, that would be entirely different. That might be the beginning of a permanent feeling that would ally itself with many things already established in his makeup. Might be love. Might even be love."

She looked at Alice.

Alice looked a little terrified by the large vista suddenly opened before her.

I, too, was frightened by this sudden opening into worlds that were new to me. What does one do about it, I thought. What should Alice do about it? If a man squeezed your hand was it up to you to determine whether that squeeze was an isolated squeeze or one of indefinite and endless boundaries?

I knew one thing.

If ever I had a love affair in Paris, I'd never let a Stein know it. I felt there would be nothing left to it after it passed these ponderous judgments.

In some way all the fun of Picasso's squeeze had been squeezed out.

Supper in Montmartre

Picasso and Fernande were giving a supper to Rousseau. They called it an *homage*.

Rousseau was the darling of the Montmartre group of painters. He was a douanier and had never received instruction in painting. He painted trees and plants and animals that had never grown anywhere. I liked to look at his paintings, although they did not look like anything I had ever seen. I wanted one for myself to take home. I liked his trees more than paintings of real trees. Everybody loved Rousseau. Everyone smiled when they spoke of his paintings, as if they were patting him on the shoulder. Not as if he were a real artist, more like a little brother who painted things in a way that made everybody tender towards him.

Henri (Le Douanier) Rousseau, photographed by Pablo Picasso, 1910. © 2010 Estate of Pablo Picasso/Artists Rights Society (ARS), New York. Musée Picasso Paris. Photo Credit: Réunion des Musées Nationaux/Art Resource, NY

We entered upon great excitement. Men and women were walking about the atelier. Fernande met us at the door.

"Nothing has come," she cried, "not a thing. Féix Potin promised to have everything here at the house at four o'clock. There is nothing for supper, absolutely nothing. Nothing has come," she repeated, "and the shop is closed." She walked up and down the room frantically appealing to one guest after the other. Everyone talked at once.

"Why not rouse somebody at Félix Potin's?"

"Too late, much too late. The store is locked."

Picasso came to a decision. "We will all go out and find food here in Montmartre. The girls can stay here and wait. We'll go out and buy food and bring it home."

They left in a body. Picasso, Leo, Braque, Apollinaire, André Salmon.

"Let me have your hats," said Fernande, and she took the brown and yellow felt sailor hat from Gertrude, and my turban with a cluster of roses, to another room.

Fernande never stopped her abuse of Félix Potin. She opened the window and looked out. We could see the men going from shop to shop. Finally they returned carrying packages. The women opened them. Bread, butter, cheese, sliced meats, bottles of wine. Everybody sat down at the table. Fernande commanded and we found our chairs. Leo drew his violin from its case. Braque placed his accordion

before him. Marie Laurencin took a seat beside Apollinaire, who held a manuscript in his hand. At the head of the table, in the chair of honor, raised high on a platform, Rousseau sat, smiling at the faces before him.

A tall, refined looking young man took his seat beside me at the lower end. He was André Salmon, who had been introduced to me as a poet. I liked his looks and his quiet speaking voice. As he spoke I mentally invited him to tea. He spoke to me of his verses. He would like to send me a book of his verses if I would care to have a copy. When I told him of my home in California, he told me of a curious experience which always accompanied his approach to an unfamiliar city. Before he arrived in a new place, he said, the city appeared to him in all detail, clear as in vision. It was an unfailing occurrence. Had I ever had such an experience? No, I never had. The idea of it struck me as uncommon, perhaps it was mystical. I would like to know him better. We drank to each other. Mentally I changed my invitation to him. I would ask him to dinner rather than to tea.

"You people down there," Picasso called to us. "You are too serious. Wake up." He raised his glass. "Salmon, wake up, a toast!" he cried.

I looked towards Salmon. He was no longer beside me. He was standing on the table opposite Braque, a raised glass in his hand. "To Braque," he cried, in a new hoarse voice. "A toast to my old friend Braque." He emptied his

glass, jumped off the table, and ran from the room. The door slammed behind him. "There he goes," Marie Laurencin called to my open-mouthed bewilderment. "He should never have drunk that second glass. He knows he cannot stand more than one."

Through the window we could see the disappearing coattails of the poet, running down the hill.

Too bad, I thought, just when I was about to invite him to dinner.

No one paid any more attention to the vanished poet. Apollinaire rose. From his pocket be drew a roll of paper. He turned to Rousseau and read aloud verses he had written, verses of tender appreciation. The eyes of the artist filled as he listened.

Silence followed, broken by Braque, who began to play. As he played, he drew notes of singular sweetness from his accordion, Leo accompanying him on his violin. Verses, violin, and accordion each added a note of the love that each man present directed to the young painter seated in the chair of honor at the head of the table. Suddenly Picasso called to me.

"You," he cried. "Sing us a song, a song from America."

Everyone turned to me, and waited.

"I cannot," I pleaded. "I don't sing."

"Any song, you must know one song. 'The hymn of Indian Territory,'" Apollinaire cried. "Sing us that!"

"Yes, sing us 'The Hymn of Indian Territory.'" They all turned to me.

I looked helplessly at Alice. She nodded encouragement.

What could I do? I couldn't sing. There was no "Hymn of Indian Territory."

Out of the nowhere rang the old familiar command, "Give them the Oski!" At once I knew that the college yell of my student days would be completely right, completely appropriate.

Without hesitation, I rose to my feet. I cried boldly:

"Oski wow wow
Whisky wee wee
Ole Muck I
Ole Ber-kely i
California
Wow!"

The full applause of Montmartre rewarded me. Gertrude beamed her approval. To this day I have never relinquished the memory of myself on my feet shouting the yell of the University of California and the enthusiastic reception of Montmartre.

At the end of the dinner, on our way out of the Picasso apartment, we stopped in the anteroom to collect our coats and hats. I picked up my turban. It had undergone complete transformation. The leaves of the roses had

been chewed off. Everybody looked at everybody. Marie Laurencin looked out of the window toward the street. Apollinaire opened his lips, then closed them, having said nothing.

Two weeks later Leo and Gertrude gave a return party to the Picassos. The same people were present whom we had met in Montmartre. I was seated alone on one side of the atelier when André Salmon came in. He came directly to me. His mien was as elegant as on the night when I first met him.

"I want to apologize to you for my unpardonable performance," he said. "I want to assure you that what happened that night has never happened to me before in all my life. The hat, the velvet roses. I will never forgive myself."

I looked from him to the other guests in the room. Before each chair a man was kneeling, his eyes upon a woman seated above him. Each man was addressing to the woman the same words that Salmon was saying to me.

"I assure you, Mlle," each man was saying, "Such a thing never occurred to me before in all my life."

"Don't speak of it," I said to Salmon. "Forget it."

He sat down beside me.

When I looked up again, I saw a procession approaching. Picasso headed it, a sword in his hand which he had detached from the wall. Each man held a weapon. The procession stopped in front of Salmon.

"We are a rescue party," Pablo explained. "The last time you two met she had a terrible effect upon you. We've come to rescue you, come!"

He drew Salmon from the chair beside me and the procession marched away, out of the room.

Modigliani, Picasso, and André Salmon in front the Café de la Rotonde, Paris, 1916. Modigliani Institut Archives Légales, Paris-Rome.

Fiesole: Sarah Heals Me

All the while that I was having my portrait done by Edstrom in Paris, I was not seeing the Steins at all. I had lost connection with Sarah and Mike because of my interest in Gertrude. And then I lost connection with Gertrude because of an exclusive interest in Edstrom. It was because of my physical need and the growing friendship of Alice and Gertrude that our relations were renewed.

Summer came.

Alice and I rented a villa opposite Villa Bardi, which the Steins had taken for the summer. It was called Casa

Alice B. Toklas and Harriet Levy at Fiesole, 1909. Courtesy of The Bancroft Library, University of California, BANC PIC 1964.049—ALB.

Ricci. It was on top of a hill in the midst of a lovely garden.

Every morning we would go down into Florence and make purchases, often of old furniture and pieces of old jewelry, and return with a prize. A credenza, a cobbler's table, or if one's luck was good, a hand-tooled chair or a bronze mortar.

When I visited a gallery with Gertrude, an old painting or a bronze would release a beauty invisible to me when I went alone. It was because of this certainty of a gift to myself that I loved to go about with Gertrude or Leo.

After a morning of successful shopping, we returned to the villa in time to escape the extreme heat of the summer and found relaxation by stretching our bodies on the cool floors.

With our arrival in Fiesole, Gertrude came into my life again. On the first day she hurried down our hill to meet me. With no prelude she began:

"Are you in love with Edstrom?"

"No."

"Is he in love with you?"

"No."

So ended Gertrude's mental unrest and the intestinal disturbance that always accompanied the presence in her mind of any unsatisfied curiosity.

Gertrude Stein and Alice B. Toklas in Venice, 27 March 1908.
Courtesy of The Bancroft Library, University of California, California Faces: Stein, Gertrude, 1874–1946:1.

Sarah took with poor grace what she called my desertion of her for Gertrude. There was tension between us.

It was in Fiesole that the friendship between Alice and Gertrude began.

Gertrude came to the house every day. This was the beginning of a friendship that was to last for thirty years.

Alice wept and she wept.

Day after day she wept because of the new love that had come into her life.

Alice used thirty handkerchiefs a day.

One day Gertrude said that she had told Sarah that she must heal me of my not being able to walk.

Sarah was so angry at me that she refused to come to our villa. Gertrude persuaded her to come.

She came each morning, her tight little face looking unfamiliar, like a stranger.

She sat outside of our villa and talked about God.

She talked about the love of God for His children. Of how He wouldn't possibly deprive His child of any good. Of the capacity He had given me to walk and do anything that was necessary for my happiness.

She talked as one does to a child. Words of one syllable.

As she talked, what she said sounded simple and real.

At night I thought of it.

It wasn't like words from a book.

It had nothing to do with Mrs. Eddy and *Science and Health*.

It was just facts about a Father and His love for His children.

I saw it and accepted it as such.

I thought of physicians I had known. And told myself that any doctor who could help a patient overcome a handicap of any kind could help her. He couldn't mind helping her.

My world became a simple world of family relations. Father-child. A loving Father.

I thought of the love of God that I had felt in Paris and I knew that God would not deny help to His child. It became unreasonable that He would not help me to walk. A simple natural gift He had given to all His children. I had the feeling that I *was* able to walk.

In the morning the certainty of being able to walk remained with me and I started out on the road that led from our villa. I walked easily for two miles before I returned, beat. There was nothing spectacular about it. I just walked naturally. I had always walked. I walked over to the Villa Bardi and told Sarah that I could walk.

It was the first time I had walked to their place. The news was accepted without astonishment. I did not see anyone but Sarah that morning.

Up to that time I had not walked without distress for eight years.

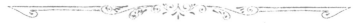

Two days later I was again unable to walk.

I drove over to Sarah and told her.

She was red with rage.

She looked at me as at one who had betrayed her and said, "Nothing like that. You walk. For the first time I have convinced Gertrude and Leo of the Truth of Christian Science Healing. The first time they have had any confidence in me as a practitioner. Don't you dare to go back on me. Now walk!" she said and pushed me out of the house.

I walked home and have been walking ever since.

After that Sarah and I were friends again.

Later on, in Paris, Gertrude reproached me because nothing had happened to me as a result of my spiritual experience.

She said, "St. Francis did not receive half as much as you and look what he did and how it changed him."

I just accepted the reproach.

She was bothered by the fact that there had been no change in me, no transformation in my character, just the miraculous fact of my being able to walk.

Neither Gertrude nor Leo ever again spoke to me about my walking. It was just accepted. I never asked Gertrude what she thought of it. I didn't ask her if it changed her feelings about Christian Science. I didn't connect God with it. I didn't connect a spiritual experience with it.

Sarah and Christian Science helped me to walk, I said. Sarah was a Christian Science practitioner who healed by means of Christian Science. She healed me of not being able to walk. I couldn't walk before and now I could walk. That was all I thought about it.

Christ healed many, I recalled, and only one turned to thank him.

Everyone who has known me intimately has remarked on my capacity for ingratitude.

I did not ask how Gertrude and Leo were affected by the healing in their appraisal of Christian Science and Sarah's devotion to it.

I did not think beyond my healing.

I could walk.

I did not credit God with the healing.

Sarah and her knowledge of Christian Science were alone in my mind associated with my recovery.

I was not grateful to God—nor to Christian Science—nor to Sarah.

No healing that I heard of then or later increased my faith in God—nor my gratitude to him.

A practitioner in Florence to whom I went told me that it was difficult to maintain a spiritual attitude of mind in Fiesole because of the monastery.

The monastery was right on the hill above Casa Ricci.

This Christian Scientist told me that the priests

in their cells at night worked against the influence of Christian Science thought.

One night I couldn't sleep.

I rose and sat before my window.

The moonlight flooded the garden.

I looked across at the monastery and thought of the priests in their cells.

I said to myself, In every cell there is a priest working against little Harriet.

I did not believe a word of it.

As I sat there meditating on the evil intentions of the priests, I heard a bird sing below me in the garden. It was unlike anything I had ever heard. It was hardly singing. It was more like a voice telling the history of its people, telling the saga of its race.

A story was being unfolded.

It began. Stopped. Was renewed and continued.

I knew without being told that I was listening to a nightingale. The song was unlike any other song.

Pure.

Beautiful.

Unlike anything I had ever heard or was ever to hear.

After that night I heard other nightingales sing, but never again did I have the same sense of a narrative, of a recitative telling the story of a race.

I have never forgotten it.

My ears that night were opened. But I felt no gratitude for that. I was not even affected by the fact that I felt no gratitude.

It was all this which disturbed Gertrude.

I am not trying to draw any deduction.

I only set down the fact that though acted upon by all these events I seemed impervious to them.

Nothing happened to me.

Mildred Aldrich

Hardly a day passed but Mildred Aldrich appeared in the house of Gertrude or in our house.

Always in the heat of an emotion. Always with a telegram in her hand and the urge to share its contents.

She had just received a wire from her American theatrical agent that needed to be answered. Mildred had either wired a question, or the answer to a question.

Mildred Aldrich bought French plays for the American market. This had been her occupation for years.

Above all our friends, she was the most social.

Her home was frequented by leaders of the stage, actors and writers. In those days actors and actresses of note were not visited in their hotels by newspaper reporters. The

newspaper writer remained in her own home and interviewed them. Mildred was one of the most distinguished newspaper reviewers. To go to her home to tea was to meet celebrities of the American stage and playwrights. She had instituted dramatic interviews from Booth to Margaret Anglin.

When she came to Paris to live, the world of the theatre followed her to her apartment. She had what approached a salon of distinction, more closely than anyone I knew.

When I came to Paris she had just bought *The Blue Bird* of Maeterlinck and was about to go to London to witness the first performance of the play.

One day Mildred Aldrich came to the house and announced that she was about to leave Paris.

She said that she was tired of struggling, of trying to live her life within the earnings from the purchase of French plays for the American market as she had been doing for many years. She would retire to a French village, not too far from Paris, furnish a small cottage, and spend the remainder of her life free from financial strain, living within her annuities.

We told her that the idea was a mad one.

At this time she was 60 years old. Her plan to leave Paris and live the remainder of her days in seclusion shocked us. She was pre-eminently social and we could not associate her with village life, removed from the scene, from people of note, above all things the stage. It would mean the end of her active life and her writing, which had been growing less vital

over the years. She was still a vigorous woman, sturdy, eager, equipped to cope with life. Her friends tried to dissuade her from her plan to retire.

She listened to none of us. She was tired. Tired of the fights. Quiet was what she was seeking for the remainder of her days.

And so she bought the home of a peasant in Huiry, about thirty miles from Paris, furnished it with her belongings, dissolved all her Paris connections, and settled in the village.

Came the First World War.

The village of Huiry was evacuated under the order of the British commander. Along with the other inhabitants Mildred Aldrich was advised to leave. The hill on which she lived was in the direct line of march of the German army. British officers explained to her that her home stood between the fire of the Germans and the British.

Mildred refused to leave. She said that she would be of some service to the British.

All the foreigners left Huiry except Mildred Aldrich.

The Battle of the Marne was fought in front of her cottage.

That was her retirement from life.

She did serve the British (making a home for the officers).

She wrote her book *A Hilltop on the Marne* in her cottage.

It was the first book to come out of the war.

Later she wrote two more books.

It was during this time that she wrote me "———".

The hilltop on the Marne became like a shrine.

Years ago when she died, Gertrude Stein wrote to me and said, "I was with Mildred Aldrich in the hospital when she died. She died sincerely, as she had lived."

She was fearless and followed her warm impulses freely without any regard for public opinion or public feeling of the moment.

When Oscar Wilde's body was carried to the grave Mildred was one of the five or six who followed him.

When the Mona Lisa was stolen from the Louvre the papers reported that every day an American woman brought a basket of flowers and placed it in the vacant space where Mona Lisa had hung. Mildred was the American woman.

She loved Gertrude Stein, who was devoted to her, and often repeated the hope that before she died someone would attest to the absurdity of Gertrude's writings, which she would never accept as authentic.

She was extravagant and emotional in her taste.

While she was repeating to us the cables which she was sending to her dramatic agent in New York, we used to count up and translate the words into dollars, and thought of the cost of the cablegram.

When her money was at its lowest ebb she sent perfume shields to her sister for Christmas.

A Beautiful Girl

I was writing a letter at one of the tables in the lobby of the small Hôtel de Calais.

When I looked up, it was into the eyes of a young woman—standing before me.

She smiled.

"I've been wanting to talk to you for several days," she said. "You remind me so much of a woman with whom I have been travelling. I left her only yesterday. I cannot tell you how much you remind me of her."

She smiled down upon me engagingly and I returned her smile.

"It all came about by chance. I met her also in a hotel.

Right away she liked me and asked me to continue her voyage with her. She was going to Berlin."

What a charming young woman, I thought.

She wore her clothes of style—smartly—with an air and her blonde hair curled around her forehead. Her accent was German.

Something about her suggested the stage.

"You are an actress?" I asked.

"A singer, how you know?" she said. "Light opera. You know the Vienna Opera House? I sing there. You are so like my friend. Moderne. She also was moderne. We travelled together for several months. We were very happy together."

Her blue eyes invited me.

"I have a good voice. Mezzo. When I am on vacation I am free to travel. I am free to travel now."

She smiled again.

Again I knew I was being invited.

"You are alone in Paris?" she asked. "You are free?"

I arose from my chair.

"Moderne," she said. "So moderne."

Again I was conscious of an invitation.

She smiled broadly and I realized that she was very pretty.

What was she saying to me? I did not know. And at the same time I did know. I knew. And I grew tense with

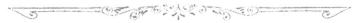

knowing that I must not let her know that I knew. I must not let her suspect that I knew.

"You live in Vienna?" I asked. I spoke quickly.

"Yes."

"With your mother?" I pursued.

She nodded.

"You have sisters? Younger sisters?"

She nodded again.

"How pleasant," I said. "How pleasant to belong to a family and have younger sisters whom you love and who love you. Are they also singers?"

"No. I am the only one," she said.

"They must be very proud of you. They and your mother. And your father? You have a father?"

"No. He's dead."

"Then it's just your mother and your little sisters. You must be very happy with them."

There was silence.

She looked at me and paused in what she was about to say. As she looked at me the smile died out of her eyes.

Suddenly she grabbed my hand and kissed it. She kissed it several times.

"Oh, pardon me. Oh, pardon me, madame," she said.

Then she was gone.

I hurried to the elevator.

I was frightened.

Nothing had been said.

Yet I was deeply moved. Depths of my being had been stirred. Stirred by fear of the question which had not been asked.

Then the question arose.

Why had she selected me?

Portrait: "The Great"

After fifteen years of absence I returned to Paris. I was eager to see Gertrude, to show her writings that I had done and hear what she had to say about it. The day of my arrival in France I found a note from her. Ford Madox Ford and his wife were having dinner with her that night. It was too bad. However, it might amuse me to meet them and we could talk afterwards, after they left.

I had waited months to show my story to Gertrude and was restless during the dinner. They left about eleven. My moment had come.

I looked up to Gertrude, ready to speak of my book. But Gertrude spoke first. "I am great," Gertrude said.

"But you were great fifteen years ago," I protested.

"No, that was only to the English-speaking people. Now France knows and honors me. I'm recognized by France."

She continued to speak about her personal affairs. There was never an opening for me to insert my story. I never got the chance to read her my story and left Paris eventually enriched only by the knowledge that Gertrude Stein was now great in France.

Gertrude Stein, date unknown. Courtesy of The Bancroft Library, University of California, California Faces: Stein, Gertrude, 1874–1946:14.

David Edstrom, *Portrait of Miss Levy*, c. 1907-8. Terra-cotta, 10.125 inches x 9.75 inches x 8.25 inches (25.7 cm x 24.8 cm x 21 cm), San Francisco Museum of Modern Art, Bequest of Harriet Lane Levy.

About the Author

Harriet Lane Levy was born into a wealthy Jewish family in San Francisco in 1867 and graduated from the University of California at Berkeley at a time when women graduates were relatively uncommon. In the 1890s she wrote for the groundbreaking journal *The Wave*, along with Jack London and Frank Norris. After serving as the drama critic for the *San Francisco Call* she moved to Paris, where she became part of a circle that included Gertrude Stein, Pablo Picasso, Georges Braque, and Henri Matisse. From her return to California at the beginning of World War I until her death in 1950, she led a life of eccentricity and independence, residing in luxury hotels in San Francisco and Carmel, attended by suitors and admirers. She is the author of *920 O'Farrell Street*, an affectionate and vivid account of her childhood in San Francisco.

HEYDAY

into California

About Heyday

Heyday is an independent, nonprofit publisher and unique cultural institution. We promote widespread awareness and celebration of California's many cultures, landscapes, and boundary-breaking ideas. Through our well-crafted books, public events, and innovative outreach programs we are building a vibrant community of readers, writers, and thinkers.

Thank You

It takes the collective effort of many to create a thriving literary culture. We are thankful to all the thoughtful people we have the privilege to engage with. Cheers to our writers, artists, editors, storytellers, designers, printers, bookstores, critics, cultural organizations, readers, and book lovers everywhere!

We are especially grateful for the generous funding we've received for our publications and programs during the past year from foundations and hundreds of individual donors. Major supporters include:

Anonymous; James Baechle; Bay Tree Fund; B.C.W. Trust III; S. D. Bechtel, Jr. Foundation; Barbara Jean and Fred Berensmeier; Berkeley Civic Arts Program and Civic Arts Commission; Joan Berman; Peter and Mimi Buckley; Lewis and Sheana Butler; California Council for the Humanities; California Indian Heritage Center Foundation; California State Library; California Wildlife Foundation/California Oak Foundation; Keith Campbell Foundation; Candelaria Foundation; John and Nancy Cassidy Family Foundation, through Silicon Valley Community Foundation; The Christensen Fund; Compton Foundation; Lawrence Crooks; Nik Dehejia; George and Kathleen Diskant; Donald and Janice Elliott, in honor of David Elliott, through Silicon Valley Community Foundation; Federated Indians of Graton Rancheria; Mark and Tracy Ferron; Furthur Foundation; The Fred Gellert Family Foundation; Wallace Alexander Gerbode Foundation; Wanda Lee Graves and Stephen Duscha; Walter & Elise Haas Fund; Coke and James Hallowell; Carla Hills; Sandra and Chuck Hobson; James Irvine Foundation; JiJi Foundation; Marty and Pamela Krasney; Guy Lampard and Suzanne Badenhoop; LEF Foundation; Judy McAfee; Michael McCone; Joyce Milligan; Moore Family Foundation; National Endowment for the Arts; National Park Service; Theresa Park; Pease Family Fund, in honor of Bruce Kelley; The Philanthropic Collaborative; PhotoWings; Resources Legacy Fund; Alan Rosenus; Rosie the Riveter/WWII Home Front NHP; The San Francisco Foundation; San Manuel Band of Mission Indians; Savory Thymes; Hans Schoepflin; Contee and Maggie Seely; Stanley Smith Horticultural Trust; William Somerville; Stone Soup Fresno; James B. Swinerton; Swinerton Family Fund; Thendara Foundation; Tides Foundation; TomKat Charitable Trust; Lisa Van Cleef and Mark Gunson; Whole Systems Foundation; John Wiley & Sons; Peter Booth Wiley and Valerie Barth; Dean Witter Foundation; and Yocha Dehe Wintun Nation.

Board of Directors

Getting Involved

To learn more about our publications, events, membership club, and other ways you can participate, please visit www.heydaybooks.com.